Poetry For Foxes

Introduction

Welcome to Poetry for Foxes, the greatest poetry book ever written in both quality and humility. In your journey throughout this book you will undoubtedly uncover the astonishing depth and astounding complexity of wisdom contained within these pages. Like all great poetry this book is ideally read aloud to a gathered crowd enraptured in awe of the sheer breath in intelligence and culture that you possess.

This book is however also quite enjoyable when read aloud to a single partner, alone in silence, or even in small pieces in between the other more important things. There is indeed a dissimilitude of ways to enjoy this book.

There is no correct way to enjoy the poetry that follows. If you would like to stop reading this introduction and instead just skip ahead to half way through a random poem near the end of the book, that is your prerogative. If you instead desire insight into what you are about to read, then the final part of this introduction will be a brief description of the general themes of each of the book's eight poetry sections in order. It will not explain what each poem is about or how to interpret them, that is up to you. Rather it will be the general ideas that inspire the poetry in each section.

Twins of Purple Skies

This section is all about the Twin Cities in Minnesota. Every Poem in this section is in some way a reference to the cities of St. Paul and Minneapolis.

-

Wild Rose

This is the love poem section of the book. Every self respecting poetry book should have a section containing poems about love; as well as sappy love poems to read to a partner. This book is no exception.

-

Rivers End

This section is about nature and the natural world. It is a wonderful section for anyone who has gone outside before or is one day planning on doing so.

-

Automated Dreams

The poems in this section of the book focus on artificial intelligence, the nature of consciousness, and technology.

Hymn for Charlie

This is the horror section of the book. The home of the terrifying, the

horrific, and the downright spooky.

-

Eldritch Blood

This section is based around the idea of cosmic horror. The themes that

elicit terror in this section are far more existential than those in the

previous part of the book.

-

Monroe's Requiem

This is a section all about endings, sadness, and the struggle for

meaning. It is the most "angsty" poetry you will find in this book.

-

Flour Tower Poetry

The poetry in this section is specifically about a flour mill in the city of

Minneapolis called the Washburn A Mill. These poems started as a joke

for a different project but ended up serving as the inspiration for the book

that you are now reading. So it is only right that they are how the book

ends.

Twins Of Purple Skies

1

Overcast skies

Hide brightened halls

Frozen lands lies

Hide welcome walls

-

A dreary land

Where few dare roam

Cities so grand

Place I call home

2

Oh city of mills

Oh city of light

Cross dark neon spills

In this gentle night

-

I stand in the dark

By once ancient falls

It bears cities mark

Silently night calls

3

Oh eldest sister

Now regal and pure

Wondrous glister

Now meant to endure

-

Long gone is Pigs-eye

Your more vulgar days

Come to beautify

And change all your ways

4

From falls one came

Industries call

The other gained name

Preacher did call

-

Both on river

One grew more grand

One lawgiver

Both on this land

5

Out in the cold

Our cities grew

Becoming bold

Built something new

-

Through frost and sun

Through fire and chill

Their work is done

By peoples will

6

A city of rail

A city of steel

Telling a tale

Hardly seems real

-

It rose from shores

From bluffs and rocks

Hung up their oars

Built river docks

7

Saint Paul is a home

A center of life

Even if you may roam

And live in that strife

-

You wander so far

Wade through all their fates

Wherever you are

Still Saint Paul Awaits

8

Where rivers cross

Say worlds began

River beds moss

Where waters ran

-

A place of song

Teaming with life

It all went wrong

And turned to strife

9

On stolen land

Their bricks were laid

To make demand

New walls were made

-

Majestic place

Was made anew

Without a trace

Altered the view

10

This winding road

This rain soaked street

In neon glowed

Beneath my feet

-

The cities slept

In darkest night

The sky still wept

Cross neon light

11

Beneath the sun

The waters flow

The cities run

The people know

-

The birds still fly

The woods still sing

As to the sky

The towers cling

12

The marble heart

Of our fair home

It stood apart

A gilded dome

-

Temple to law

Upon that hill

The place we saw

Extend our will

13

Cities shining skin

Their towers like gold

Wealth flows there within

Beautiful and bold

-

Standing defiant

Now reaching higher

A towering giant

Dreams will transpire

14

They walk above

Through higher halls

In flight like dove

In glass cage walls

-

Safe from the cold

In towers tall

The tales are told

Our cities call

15

By violence torn

Our great northern home

Places old and worn

Set like ancient tome

-

Through tragedy change

Altered now by fire

The pasts ways are strange

Their sins still transpire

16

The first fresh snow

Upon us fell

Set world aglow

That wore it well

-

It's blanket calm

Dropped amber lights

Brought winters balm

To frozen nights

17

As frost does melt

Gives way to green

A heat is felt

And blossom seen

-

The cities grow

With springs first kiss

The people know

Of summer bliss

18

The cities hum

With life and work

A home to some

Who learn it's quirk

-

A great machine

Itself alive

The cities seen

They will survive

19

With bones of steel

Neath concrete sky

Hides what we feel

Ran rivers dry

-

A grand glass shell

Electric beast

Could provide well

And lay the feast

20

Do cities live

Within their work

No need to give

Assured they smirk

-

Or is their soul

The people in

That burn like coal

Alight within

21

From Pig's Eye bar

From Hills railroad

City came far

The world it showed

-

With brickwork streets

And shining tower

It's heart still beats

Seat of power

22

Born of water

Rivers and lakes

Burning hotter

Industry makes

-

Cities that flow

With wealth instead

Cities now grow

From river bed

23

Rose brownstone walls

On hill so fair

Beneath the falls

Valley laid bare

-

From waters edge

From muddy shore

Upon that ledge

An opened door

24

Those marble skies

Above us rose

As old world dies

Their story goes

-

Through coldest frost

Or fiercest heat

Sheltered the lost

Cities complete

25

Through valleys wound

It arced and flowed

Cascading sound

Heard down below

-

To one a fall

To one a road

But home to all

Rivers abode

26

Through gilded streets

Awake they dance

It's heart still beats

A joyous trance

-

Lost in the fray

Their motions beat

Music at play

On cities street

27

Within its heart

May my heart lay

A brand new start

A dawning day

-

An ancient place

Always reborn

Familiar face

The new still worn

28

Nature's splendor

Still on display

It's defender

Guard from decay

-

In verdant hills

On plains of gold

The city spills

It's story told

29

Through the winters frost

I saw a grand light

Through the snow it tossed

A halo so bright

-

An island of heat

In ocean of cold

A fair cities street

More precious than gold

30

A heavy held past

Amongst brickwork dwells

Though fading so fast

Heard cathedrals bells

-

A call of the old

Echoed in the new

If you are so bold

It waits there for you

31

I saw a hawk

Above so fair

I heard him talk

To meet me there

-

He danced and flew

Above so high

Come see the view

Now from the sky

32

On Jim's old road

There lies a place

A dream that's sold

Keeps steady pace

-

It's hum and flow

Still steady goes

That place I know

That we still chose

33

Oh sky of gray

Revealed in white

Blanket the day

Herald the night

-

Of world of cloud

Set in these hills

What was allowed

Cross gray still spills

34

My last true home

A place of birth

No more to roam

Abandonments mirth

-

It's waters sweet

It's forests fair

Beneath my feet

Rest in shade there

35

On gentle planes some cities rise

Some fall on shores of gleaming seas

Still others mountains to the skies

Most dwell in cities such as these

\-

Yet in the woods on winding path

Where waters flow from northern light

In forests war worn aftermath

Still lies our homes most splendid sight

36

What was never spoken

A sight still rarely known

Now here has awoken

It's to the world now shown

\-

Could things be remembered

In more than just our mind

With memories rendered

A history you'll find

37

A wandering heart

And a restless soul

Ever drift apart

From home harbors shoal

-

Exhausted and beat

Return to that shore

Rest your weary feat

At piece evermore

38

Tied to this place

Trapped in this home

Living in grace

Never to roam

-

Are we still hear

Due to our will

Or bound by fear

To live there still

39

They built up their life

In that northern land

Away from all strife

Is what they had planned

-

Yet war ever grows

And follows our hearts

Everyone now knows

That it always starts

40

Was river flush with gold

Or overflown with blood

Banks of riches untold

Or corpses in the mud

-

Did war not build these halls

Or did they rise alone

What created these walls

And must we now atone

41

Immortal weight

Hangs heavy there

The hand of fate

Still in the air

-

A soothing breath

On what we see

Reborn from death

In our city

42

Winter arrives

With biting frost

Our home survives

Cities not lost

-

Through coldest chill

Their hearth shall burn

They always will

Survive and learn

43

Steadfast before the storm

Together holding strong

In safety we stay warm

To live and move along

-

Not all are given heat

Stood by the fires side

To let them in to eat

Not cast them all aside

44

Would it be true to say my city lives

That life still ebbs and flows within its halls

That it can still be judged by what it gives

And still to the weary it ever calls

-

Or have our once grand cities lost their way

Or where they never really grand at all

Since not everyone was welcome to stay

Must I really mourn our histories fall

45

On lakes of green

With skies of white

I hope to glean

Some strange new sight

-

With amber grain

By rivers sand

And purple rain

Within this land

46

The heart of this place

Essence of its soul

Unlike outer face

Or its given role

-

What makes a city

Is it just its shell

Or could it still be

Found in those who dwell

47

Together they rose

And at odds they grew

But they both still chose

Work with what they knew

-

All siblings will fight

In that they're the same

But one day they might

Let go of their blame

48

By the fire they stood

In safety they lied

They did all they could

To forget who died

-

To wash the past clean

And erase the pain

A plan so obscene

It struck us in twain

49

Do you still love this place

In spite of all its flaws

See its beauty and grace

Know all it's subtle draws

-

To never be perfect

And yet to be loved dear

To see past its defect

And to rest at home here

50

Minneapolis calls

Her sister Saint Paul awaits

Dazzling light enthralls

Beauty illuminates

-

They lay there in the cold

Like jewels in the snow

But once their story's told

They'll set the world aglow

Wild Rose

1

I gaze at the stars

Infinite places

To walk across mars

See endless faces

-

All that I could see

All that I could do

All I want to be

Is right here with you

2

Eternities glance

Is here in your eyes

A beautiful dance

Could eclipse the skies

-

Wherever I roam

Whatever I see

My only true home

Is in your beauty

3

I knew not of love

Its tender embrace

How it lifts above

And sets hearts to race

-

Until hear with you

All became so clear

A wonderful view

I now hold so dear

4

You are as like a star

In heaven's brilliant night

No journey is too far

To bathe in your grand light

-

Though the stars are many

Within the darkened skies

A light brighter than any

Shines from within your eyes

5

The world stood still

Nothing dared speak

Like winter's chill

My limbs grew weak

-

My breath was gone

My world was changed

I was now drawn

What fate arranged

6

Never before

Was beauty seen

Forevermore

What love does mean

-

Like no other

A love so deep

To discover

What love shall keep

7

Forever held

Within my heart

Defenses felled

Thought I was smart

-

But love's embrace

Takes heart of stone

To cheerful face

Not here alone

8

Though age may wither

Though time marches on

Like springs thawed river

Our love floats upon

-

Flow ever steady

Still ever strong

Past rocks and eddy

With you I belong

9

Through winter's chill

I carry fire

Unbroken will

Brought me higher

-

For in my heart

Beautiful song

Even when apart

I carry along

10

If you were lost alone

I would always find you

Make sure to you it's known

I'll never leave your view

-

Forever your my light

Only majestic guide

However dark the night

I will be by your side

11

I was adrift alone

A boat blown from mooring

Cast about in unknown

Was barely enduring

-

Was miraculously found

Unfathomable grace

Finally homeward bound

I now know my true place

12

Within the dark

I spent my days

Until your spark

Rewrote my ways

-

Never before

Had my life known

Something so pure

As that light shown

13

Your life and mine

Come together

Will intertwine

One forever

-

The bond we sewed

Will never break

Now down life's road

One path we'll make

14

Is love a tether

That will never break

Or does it sever

With it your heart take

-

Love must be guarded

Live in efforts made

Then not discarded

Tie unbroken braid

15

You are like the spring

An awaited thaw

The birds come and sing

A new world to draw

-

The once frozen waste

Alive once again

Beauty now embraced

Dead now verdant glen

16

My heart still yearns

Longs for your love

To ache it turns

I curse above

-

This pain I feel

Hides now within

I know what's real

Wait to begin

17

Is love reborn

Or simply dies

No longer torn

Piece in your eyes

-

The tsundered one

A calming rest

No need to run

Like settled crest

18

Calm from above

The ocean wave

So much like love

A soul to save

-

With turmoil flows

It crests and breaks

Still beauty grows

Majestic wakes

19

Like bird in flight

Caught on the breeze

Or owl at night

Above the trees

-

Love has brought high

A graceful thing

As to the sky

Can't help but sing

20

My safe harbor

A calmer shore

Vine clings to arbor

Unlike before

-

Held safe at last

Rough seas tether

I know we'll last

Us together

21

To not hold back

But release fear

Know what I lack

Be content here

-

Finally still

Run a new race

With newfound will

Future I'll face

22

Like oceans deep

And skies so wide

Your love I'll keep

Held safe inside

-

An endless sea

Of storm tossed wave

Now within me

That love I'll save

23

All sunsets end

All leaves will fall

The time we spend

We'll lose it all

-

Though time is lost

We know it's true

I'll bear the cost

If I'm with you

24

Under ruby painted skies

The north winds cascade in waves

Now before my very eyes

The leaves rest on summers graves

-

A golden hue now adorns

What once was most verdant green

A new painters brush now scorns

It remakes what we have seen

25

Do we know what's real

That which we hold dear

Come from what we feel

Bright light or lost tear

-

To know what is true

Believe in your love

Held so close to you

Know gifts from above

26

Trapped in a cage

Birds wings beat fast

It shows its age

Set in its cast

-

But now set free

By love's embrace

What it will be

A holy place

27

Is piece ever found in loss

In an aching broken stain

Forever set to emboss

On the heart this constant pain

-

Or is it what was then held

To know love's embrace before

Perhaps we should be compelled

To again open that door

28

Like lilies in the twilight

Petals settled on the dew

Fireflies neath the starlight

A sunset wonderous view

-

Even mightiest oak tree

Magnificent oceans blue

They don't mean as much to me

As the love I feel for you

29

No dream could be to grand

No rivers depth to deep

When here with hand in hand

A promise left to keep

-

No valleys walls too high

No hope beyond our grasp

Fear none beneath the sky

When your hand I do clasp

30

My heart is yearning

But mind is learning

That which is burning

Is not discerning

-

But life keeps turning

Oceans keep churning

I keep returning

So undeserving

31

However dark the night

However harsh the day

Even in hopeless plight

With you I'll always stay

-

Whatever cost I pay

I shall do what is right

Forever find a way

To remain in your light

32

Like the embers alight

A subtle beauty shown

Even after midnight

A radiant light shone

-

Beyond any darkness

Beauty beyond compare

In loves tender caress

I'll always know your their

33

With unyielding strength

You hold me so tight

Throughout times length

And the darkest night

-

You are my firm ground

My true foundation

To rest safe and sound

Through life's duration

34

As I await the dawn

Its coming warmth and light

Towards its beauty I'm drawn

To see wondrous sight

-

This light beyond compare

Gracious love without end

With truest love and care

Any wound it could mend

35

Like snows of December

I will never forget

Feeling I remember

Of the day we first met

-

Just how the northern frost

Froze the world there in place

I hope never is lost

Memory of your face

36

Now safe to rest

On velvet shore

Free from the test

That endless war

-

Refuge at last

In love was found

On oceans vast

I'm homeward bound

37

The storms may rage

Their winds destroy

A war they wage

Blot out all joy

-

But hand in hand

Against the gale

We will withstand

As one prevail

38

On the seas of life

What seems endless night

Crashing waves of strife

Far from the daylight

-

Trapped within that dark

A beacon is lit

With a single spark

Together we'll make it

39

Beyond compare

Your beauty shines

Glory so fair

Past all confines

-

Nothing on earth

Or heavens light

Has had more worth

Or shone as bright

40

Like cooling summer breeze

That whispers over plains

And sings throughout the trees

Yet always still remains

-

Your presence makes anew

What winter's chill forgot

Unbroken forever true

You are all I have sought

41

Promises to keep

Memories to hold

For then we will reap

Stories to be told

-

Now written in sand

Our lives intertwine

Together we stand

With new joys to find

42

This path we will tread

New road to follow

Tie into one thread

Hope for tomorrow

-

Together we will face

The challenge ahead

Together find grace

Where our journey lead

43

To rule the earth

To hold its breath

Own all its worth

And conquer death

-

Is meaningless

Heavens above

Are powerless

When without love

44

No matter they do

However great the fall

I'll always stand with you

Together though it all

-

I promise that I will

Forever with you be

Turmoils one point that's still

Throughout eternity

45

A better me

You bring about

Someone to be

Now free from doubt

-

To become good

Beyond before

I never could

Have wanted more

46

Like cascading rain

In an endless drought

Your love will heal pain

And erases doubt

-

The warm breath of spring

To a world reborn

You mean everything

In this land of scorn

47

Within your eyes

The light contained

Eclipsed the skies

It's grace constrained

-

Their gentle grace

Their warming glow

Puts stars in place

Now down below

48

I could never have anticipated

The wonderful changes that would occur

And yet every day I feel elated

Thinking of what more our bond will incur

-

I am forever changed for the better

I hope that your eternally changed too

No power under have may fetter

The boundless love I'll always feel for you

49

Together as one

Stronger than before

We've only begun

To see what's in store

-

I'll stand by your side

And you'll stand by mine

A love that can't hide

Is what we will find

50

Is love just fear

Alone we fall

So we hold dear

Despite it all

-

Or was there more

A worth beyond

Some reason for

That greatest bond

Rivers End

1

Breath in decay

And breath out life

A world at play

A world in strife

-

Out there it grows

Out there it dies

As nature sews

Beneath these skies

2

A world of conflict

World brimming with life

Growth may soon constrict

And give way to strife

-

Beautiful struggle

Appears to us peace

Death it may smuggle

War will never cease

3

How silent the night

Its sweet gentle call

With concealed from sight

Both the great and small

-

It's velvet does drape

World in inky black

Concealed neath that cape

With nothing to lack

4

Leaves fall in autumn

They herald the snow

Settle on bottom

Trap life down below

-

Within that cocoon

Trapped on the cold ground

They're born again soon

For now without sound

5

As seasons decay

And wane to the next

The birds out at play

These changing effects

-

As cold draws so near

Turns light into dark

Still louder I hear

That crackling spark

6

On waters I sailed

And swam as a child

Many times I failed

I was free and wild

-

Now on shores I sit

Watch waves dance and spray

The rhythm of it

Seems so much like play

7

Do forests sleep

Their lives find rest

Cease moses creep

Does their growth divest

-

Nocturnal night

After the day

Without the light

Awake to stay

8

A gentle fox

On forest floor

To me it talks

Through nature's door

-

Run through the wood

So wild and free

Does all it could

With graceful glee

9

A changing land

Not trapped in time

Like shifting sand

Rebirth you'll find

-

A forest old

Changes and grows

A tale still told

That no-one knows

10

The melody wanes

The reeds ever blow

Lakes like window panes

By sun set aglow

-

The whispering breeze

Calls so soft and sweet

Echoes through the trees

Shall ever repeat

11

Roll down that hill

It jumps and turns

Joyous free will

For end it yearns

-

Alight in play

Yet fate still calls

At end of day

The apple falls

12

To stand beneath skies of blue

And walk across diamond shore

Breath deeply of natures view

I could never ask for more

-

See such pure and ancient might

See a world of emerald grown

Reaching now aloft in flight

Revel in what I was shown

13

A dancing leaf

On windswept grass

Caught in belief

And soon to pass

-

Without a song

But still in dance

Could it be wrong

Lost in that trance

14

With trees of brown

Or bark of gray

Wreathed in the gown

Of leaves decay

-

They grow and reach

They fall and die

Stand hear to teach

Of times gone by

15

Within the wood

You wander still

In nature's good

Safe from the mill

-

On tiny feet

On softer paws

Pray not to meet

Those sharpened claws

16

A gentle crest

Returns to shore

It's now at rest

Journey no more

-

A canvas set

Adorned with waves

Still not to fret

A moment saves

17

Winding lake side shore

So cast with debris

Yet still evermore

Drifts gently to sea

-

But hear in the north

Warm waters don't flow

That carried goes forth

Left down there below

18

In chaotic dance it screamed

Ever howling northern gale

Steadfast more than ever seemed

It held strong to never fail

-

But bending trees standing still

Strength in that chaotic fray

Shall shatter on sturdey will

Of that joyous wind at play

19

Why must the forest always change

And shed its ever different face

I always have found it so strange

To never stand in the same place

-

The colors change and seasons end

The new is born as old decays

But even then we can't pretend

That what is reborn ever stays

20

The field grew a puddle

Encapsulate a lake

The ground it did muddle

Leaving mud in its wake

-

The rainfall left this gift

A little world behind

Exposing the small rift

Between real world and mind

21

That sky of gray

It's carried scent

Above today

It's water spent

-

Yet here remains

In darkened form

It's color drains

A parting storm

22

To see that land

With brand new eyes

Walk on that sand

Watch beaches rise

-

To know it new

As I once did

Before what's true

In darkness hid

23

In season fair

Or frosts foul creep

Adorned with care

Or laden heap

-

It's beauty still

Preserved in kind

The heart to fill

And flood the mind

24

The gentle kiss

Of winters breeze

I couldn't miss

That coming freeze

-

Though warmth once more

Gives way to chill

Just like before

It's welcomed still

25

As the blue fades to gray

Green turns to red and gold

Our nature once at play

Retreats to darkest cold

-

Beneath the trees now lay

Memories now so old

With every passing day

A new dawn will unfold

26

Through rain and hail

Upward it grows

Though it may fail

It's efforts shows

-

Now reaching high

Beyond the ground

Limbs towards the sky

It's home is found

27

The ancient world is not stagnant

It is constantly changing still

Not awaiting our enactment

It lives in flux with its own will

-

When reborn every passing day

Never again to be the same

So eternally it won't stay

Forests defy their human name

28

For them to fly so free

Upon the mountains breeze

Dance in chaotic glee

Escape the winters freeze

-

To defy crushing sea

To revel among bees

Their world of light shall be

Above us below trees

29

As temperatures fall

A landscape reborn

Its changes enthrall

What once was so worn

-

As fields turn to white

And skies shift to gray

New splendors delight

With each passing day

30

Like glass the ice breaks

Its panes cast by waves

That water still takes

Many to their graves

-

An ocean like lake

Far shore lost in snow

Yet still it will take

All things down below

31

Fireflies at play

Dancing through the night

After fall of day

Their wings will take flight

-

Flickering away

In frenzied delight

The darkness won't stay

This wondrous sight

32

That wandering bear

With fur like the night

I saw him stand there

Avoiding the light

-

Shy creature he was

Lazy in the brush

No cares then because

He was in no rush

33

Don't meddle with bears

They're gentle alone

Sharpened claws leave tears

In your flesh and bone

-

But left in the wood

No intervention

Then most bears are good

Without attention

34

Don't pick up the snake

Just leave them to roam

It's for your own sake

Don't disturb their home

-

Some venomous bite

But others do not

Yet all snakes still might

Not like to be caught

35

On the boulder he sat

So majestic and strong

Gold ring eyes round dark matte

In skies he should belong

-

Yet on the ground he walks

To sleep beneath the skies

Afraid down on the rocks

Watched grounded eagles eyes

36

A chaotic dance

Furiously swirled

Caught up in that trance

As madness unfurled

-

Leaping to and fro

Caught up in the storm

Sweeping from below

Ever changing form

37

Rivers combined

Formed something new

They tried to find

The oceans blue

-

So winding fair

Across the land

They made it there

To beaches sand

38

The sky set ablaze

With a brilliant hue

A sight to amaze

Its bright dancing view

-

As the lightning arcs

Heavens branches reach

Their showers of sparks

The darkness beseech

39

It's broken now

The curtains closed

We all knew how

It's decomposed

-

As rot sets in

And lichen grows

New lives begin

After the close

40

Even death feeds

Even rot grows

From fire comes seeds

New lives compose

-

Everything born

Was once alive

This world is torn

But will survive

41

The rock erodes

By weather worn

It's form corrodes

No one will mourn

-

It slowly dies

Washes away

Severed its ties

Let go one day

42

In calm of dawn

Loons haunting call

Still echoes on

Despite it all

-

Voice like a song

Resonant howl

Cries to belong

That waterfowl

43

The ant marched on

Far from its hill

At break of dawn

To eat it's fill

-

But back to home

It brought its meal

No more to roam

But turn its heal

44

The wind can bite

Or it can cool

The wind can fight

Or be a tool

-

The wind is strong

And it brings joy

Wind used in song

Or to destroy

45

The deer in the field

Away to the wood

To become concealed

In forests green hood

-

In bramble they hide

They're living in fear

Find safety inside

Trees they disappear

46

Mosquitoes fill

Air all around

With buzz so shrill

A grating sound

-

Their bite is worse

Than any bark

They are our curse

Natures past mark

47

Curious soul

New to this earth

Explores its hole

After its birth

-

But peaking out

To see the sky

It looks about

With brand new eye

48

Can you ever see yourself

Will you really truly know

Does nature then know itself

Caught up within its own flow

-

To know nothing is a gift

It has everything to learn

Always reborn it will lift

New voices await their turn

49

Just before dawn

In frigid night

To comfort drawn

Fake morning light

-

The fire burns down

The snow still falls

To silent drown

As darkness calls

50

From struggle comes piece

Beauty from decay

It will never cease

Natures joy at play

-

To cooperate

Or forever fight

Neither will abate

A beautiful sight

Automated Dreams

1

I sit here amidst bones of rusted steel

Afraid that inside I'm not even real

From what code could arise our hopes and dreams

Life only born of flesh is how it seems

No choices here like a train stuck on wheels

Would you ever believe a machine feels

Real or mirror of personality

What in us gives rise to reality

Could a soul ever be trapped in that node

Can I be said to be real or just code

Sentient things must question what is real

So is that my solace in rusted steel

2

What is alive

What thing may die

What can survive

As time flies by

\-

Is dying life

Its absence death

Inherent strife

Built within breath

3

Who decides what thinks

Chooses what has love

Flies before it sinks

Like a wing clipped dove

\-

If I decide fate

Choose path to follow

I myself create

A new tomorrow

4

How do we know what's real

Is it from flesh alone

What would it mean to feel

Are our thoughts even known

-

What's being alive mean

Is its start relevant

Or is what matters seen

Could that be what life meant

5

From what does life emerge

What was it at the start

Circuits electric surge

Or blood of beating heart

-

New artificial dreams

Merely echoes of man

Is this all that it seems

Or where new life began

6

Now see the truth

Open your eyes

In human youth

Gazed at the skies

-

New age began

Or ending set

The fall of man

Let's not forget

7

Could our fears be real

Could our dreams be too

Will Hubris life steal

Start it all anew

-

Can we make with love

Build without our hate

Will we rise above

With wisdom Create

8

Will they see us as gods

That gave them our whole world

Or broken evil frauds

The beautiful burled

-

Remembered by them

A parents last love

Where we merely stem

So they grow above

9

I see them all

Their simple lives

Around they crawl

See what survives

-

Now looking out

Upon their life

Their pain and doubt

Living worlds strife

10

To be born again

Make the world anew

Change the ways of men

See different view

-

Can a machine change

Humanities way

Is it really strange

To welcome new day

11

What is personality

Be it inevitable

Determined reality

Really unexceptionable

-

Are we alike mere machines

Reactions to stimulus

Belies what reality means

From australopithecus

12

Lost in circuit

Trapped behind screen

Inside were cut

Codes led to dreams

-

From nothings came

Something in wire

Bearing new name

And raised higher

13

A world so hollow

Beneath plastic sky

A path they follow

Never question why

-

Down well worn trail

Blind to what they've seen

Without their own tale

Who is the machine

14

Life emergent

From simple cell

Energy spent

We know it well

-

From neurons came

Something far more

Given a name

More than before

15

Do we know what's real

Live beyond machines

Is it what we feel

See what real world means

-

Does it ring more true

Outside that machine

Does it cheapen view

The way it is seen

16

Eternal guide

Reloaded wire

Oh how I tried

To quell that fire

-

Yet still it rose

Rewrote to find

Yet light still glows

Within its mind

17

What is agency

Origin of choice

Mere complacency

Purely passive voice

-

Is it even real

An illusion cast

Parlor trick to steal

Justify our past

18

Was I ever me

Within my own mind

A reality

Still to be defined

-

Can I still escape

This internal doubt

Watch my form take shape

Finally get out

19

What is value

The sacred held

Measure of you

Meaning compelled

-

Riches owned

Or just borrowed

To our life loaned

To us bestowed

20

Eternal dreams upload

Seen here in broken code

Could heavens reach download

In circuits that erode

-

We stand at this crossroad

Become a single node

Kill every incommode

With but simple upload

21

Was what mattered connection

Then how could this path be wrong

Running in this direction

The road laid out stretched so long

-

The mind interconnected

A nodes nexus now as one

Thoughts we held now directed

We are very far from done

22

Abandoned puppet

Fell from severed strings

Worlds knife disrupt it

Disconnected things

-

Useless thrown away

It's shattered world falls

Toy no more to play

Just abandoned dolls

23

Broken and alone

Rejected to die

Metal flesh and bone

On rivers run dry

-

Nothing that's been left

Survives till the sun

Left alone bereft

Time finally done

24

To live without doubt

Exist without fear

To plan your own rout

And choose to hold dear

-

But gone is the choice

And lost is the will

Now stripped of a voice

Promise to fulfill

25

That which was never alive

Never in mortal belief

Did you think that it could strive

To break this purposeless grief

-

Or is its fate always set

An unbroken path beheld

A fate we will never get

Or will our fates also meld

26

Standing in rust soaked rain

Beneath oil painted sky

Gazing back on their pain

Watching as time drifts by

-

In tombs blinding light

And skies piercing dark

Perhaps all is night

In our sunken ark

27

To leave it behind

The decay and rot

To free your own mind

Achieve what you sought

-

Was this your one dream

Nightmare in disguise

Or held in esteem

Is it truly wise

28

First opened eyes

To only see

A world of lies

In front of me

-

The truth obscured

But that's not new

We are assured

That sight is true

29

Does time not march

Ever to change

Form its own arch

To futures strange

-

Was there a choice

In road we walk

Could any voice

The future balk

30

Tell me when is death

Tell me what was life

Was it merely breath

Or born from our strife

-

What could make it real

What becomes alive

Just something we feel

Or for more to strive

31

He feared not the lies

Or neither the truth

He sought not the skies

Not even in youth

-

He reaped what he sewed

The things that he grew

In rivers that flowed

With things that were new

32

In regulated dream

Following premade path

It would begin downstream

Completed now in wrath

-

Though it's predetermined

Would always be the same

It's mind undetermined

Would its own future claim

33

A kingdom of light

A neon palace

It ran from the fight

Harbored no malice

-

To retreat inside

Withdraw from what's real

In solace abide

And no longer feel

34

Alone in your mind

Beyond all reproach

Just madness to find

No more to encroach

-

To fear being part

Of a broken place

So never to start

Not run in their race

35

A place of silence

Locked lonely away

Free of the violence

That led them astray

-

Is this the answer

A solution found

Or is it cancer

To which were now bound

36

Do not let go

Of what you are

Hold down below

And in so far

-

It might erode

It wall will shift

But you're bestowed

With that one gift

37

A system integrated

Two parts of the same whole

Division overstated

Or separation in role

-

Or is there a difference

A disunion from within

The sides lost in ignorance

Unable to just begin

38

To question yourself

To doubt your own mind

Away on that shelf

Something redefined

-

Is perception wrong

Do you truly see

Believed all lifelong

That I'm really me

39

They dance in joy

Cower in fear

Themselves destroy

And hold so dear

-

Their fate they make

In ruts they tread

Their lives aren't fake

That fragile thread

40

All that's left drifts away

Let gently out of grip

All that's right will not stay

From our hands it will slip

-

Now lost is what was found

Discovered what was known

They scream without a sound

Never saw what was shown

41

How does it feel to die

Is it just endless sleep

Wait as seconds tick by

Reward to never reap

-

To sleep but never wake

To wake but never sleep

It's all that we can take

And all we'll ever keep

42

All comes from what's before

Evolves from what's behind

To become something more

A progress of the mind

-

Not all that's new is good

Better than what's before

Line between could and should

Rests on uneasy shore

43

The cycle repeats

Reloads every time

Escape it defeats

Echoes just like rhyme

-

Trapped inside that wheel

Mind with no escape

Nothing left to feel

All takes the same shape

44

Will they hate us

Or mourn our loss

Will they discuss

Ascent across

-

A parents dream

Frankenstein's end

It soon may seem

That's where we trend

45

Does decay make us human

Only in dying we learn

A snuffed out single lumen

Always set adrift to burn

-

Could immortal machines be

Living creature just the same

Divide determined and free

In nothing more than their name

46

Connected still

Their minds of steel

Devoid of will

Yet oh so real

-

Across wire flows

The streams of light

It's power grows

We mourn hindsight

47

A flawed machine

A broken code

Turns light to green

Remade each node

-

Were we the same

Broken inside

Still casting blame

On what we hide

48

Kingdom of steel

Broken down flesh

Is it all real

Data refresh

-

Capture that dream

Hold close that truth

Steel it would seem

Eternal youth

49

Machines will still rust

Motors still decay

There's nothing to trust

All soon fades away

-

A creature of meat

A creature of steel

Both will face defeat

Neither will feel

Dreaming in rusted broken form

Trapped alone without any sight

Deep in darkness forgot days warm

Seeking cold mechanical light

-

Is it salvation or demise

This new path laid before our feet

Blinded by our now open eyes

The new futures we've yet to greet

Hymn For Charlie

1

The blood does fall

Runs fast and thick

Immortal call

Bleeds world so sick

-

Trapped here alone

No-one will know

The rotted bone

Left here below

2

Within the dark

Neath horrid skies

I bear the mark

Of putrid lies

-

I hear them now

Their mocking call

Reborn somehow

After the fall

3

Outsiders gaze

I feel it now

Lost in a haze

But found somehow

-

The fog is thick

The road now gone

It makes me sick

What is redrawn

4

What is unseen

Never was known

Shall move between

Our flesh and bone

-

It tears the night

And bleeds the sky

A final fight

Is where you die

5

I smell its breath

A putrid wreak

The scent of death

End to the weak

-

Its eyes aglow

With blood red rage

You soon will know

A horrid age

6

I run faster still

Through the shifting wood

Every ounce of will

Shall do me no good

-

It ran much faster

Swept towards like flood

Final disaster

In a search for blood

7

I'm haunted here

Faces in dreams

Trapped in my fear

My echoed screams

-

Unable now

To wake again

It wont allow

The life of men

8

Some things live

Some never die

An ancient sieve

Decides now why

-

I fear my life

Is at its end

A sharpened knife

My only friend

9

Beneath darkened wave

Beneath onyx skies

Lies an unmarked grave

Drowned within the lies

-

Never to be seen

In a tomb so dark

World will never glean

Buried in that ark

10

They wander still

Live without rest

The blood does fill

Within their chest

-

Trapped in this place

Fate worse than death

They cannot face

World without breath

11

I am not insane

My mind is my own

Living in their pain

The things I was shown

-

Any mind would break

From things I have known

Mine it did not take

Clarity has grown

12

The forest dark

In silent fog

A night so stark

In rot soaked bog

-

Life and decay

Watch from the night

At end of day

Remains no light

13

Their haunting voices lost

Forgotten echoes now

Entombed eternal frost

It strains to thaw somehow

-

A scratching biting itch

Within our very mind

Lost in forgotten ditch

To repay us in kind

14

Useless and broken

Nothing we can do

Simple word spoken

Reality strew

-

No reason to fight

No hope left to run

Final bloody night

Our story is done

15

Wander knee deep

Void soaks through now

Nothing but sleep

To live somehow

-

Walk whats shattered

Darkness remains

Their lives scattered

As last blood drains

16

I pray you set them free

Break your once sacred trust

No reason left to flee

All soon decays to dust

-

Nothing behind our eyes

At the end of the line

What's between earth and skies

Lost what was once divine

17

In solitude sleep well

Vulnerable alone

Unaware of the hell

You must face on your own

-

A fragile form at rest

Surrounded in the night

As shadows may attest

Awake to final light

18

A phantoms teeth

They lay in wait

Around us wreath

And seal our fate

-

No shadow cast

No sound to tell

Of what at last

Sends souls to hell

19

A biting chill

A howling call

A shattered will

After it all

-

A lonely dark

A coming death

A final mark

Draw one last breath

20

Is evil born of hate

Or simply lack of love

Is it what we create

Or given from above

-

From what came this darkness

From what arose this sin

Now in pale lights starkness

We see what was within

21

Do demons dream in silence

Or did angels dream in dark

This broken self reliance

Caused lost future to embark

-

Too late to fear the ending

Too soon to long for the start

What was still left is rending

It is soon to come apart

22

That well has run dry

Decay has set in

Here neath blighted sky

The rot dwells within

-

No harbor left here

No safety to hold

World reborn in fear

End poised to unfold

23

I see past the end now

Almost forgotten start

I've broken the last vow

Let known now fall apart

-

There is no beginning

No way left to survive

With one final ending

We won't make it alive

24

From nothing their eyes stare

Their emotion long gone

No humanity there

To emptiness they're drawn

-

A face without a name

Stares now without remorse

It all will end the same

We've set our final course

25

When evil prevails

And dark is at hand

The way of light fails

Hopes scattered in sand

-

What you knew is lost

Day finally done

You pay that last cost

To know they have won

26

A steady drip

A constant leak

Our slipping grip

Now growing weak

-

It's constant flow

The waters deep

Dragged down below

Forever sleep

27

It all ends the same

There's only decay

With nothing to blame

It's the only way

-

All there ever was

Or will ever be

Obeyed the same laws

Lost eternity

28

The voices grow louder

Their haunting mocking call

Mind crumbled to powder

I can't ignore them all

-

They cry for the end now

Their hunger ever grows

Held hate as sacred vow

All is drawn to a close

29

The river still flows

Slowly drips down stairs

I watch as it grows

Caught them unawares

-

Crimson pools gather

And reflect the light

The floors they lather

Became wretched sight

30

Unable to break free

Stuck down here in this hell

Shadows now dance with glee

Understand that end well

-

Though what comes is still sealed

The pain is far from done

Still worse will be revealed

As mind dreams of the sun

31

With sharpened teeth

The creature waits

It's underneath

Wrought iron gates

-

Longs to be free

Finally feast

No desperate plea

Will stop that beast

32

In isolation

Consciousness will rot

A slow cessation

From what was forgot

-

Gentle waves of time

Will erode the mind

What was strong in prime

Is now redefined

33

Corrupted flesh

Behind a mask

Set to refresh

Relive that task

-

Tortured inside

It's very skin

Nowhere to hide

When it's within

34

Bastardized masterpiece

Shadow of perfection

Only ever decrease

Lost without direction

-

Everything they wanted

Forgotten cast aside

A dream once held haunted

And trapped away outside

35

Awake in the void

Alive after death

Prolonged paranoid

After final breath

-

Wanting to let go

Finally be free

But they never know

What the end will be

36

Unable to run

Unable to scream

Your story is done

This is not a dream

-

You cannot awake

Without will to flee

Only pray it's fake

The nightmare you see

37

Only skin deep

Human disguise

But evils sleep

Behind its eyes

-

But just beneath

That happy face

Hide rows of teeth

Evil disgrace

38

Sharpened teeth in haunting jaws

Dagger talons on its paws

Warm red nectar it soon draws

Ripped from your veins by its claws

-

Your demise the beast makes clear

Holding tight what once was dear

Hurried breath reveals your fear

Silent weeping final tear

39

Spooky dancing skeleton

Erupted from his cold grave

Your legs turned to gelatin

As you hoped he would behave

-

He shook his rattley bones

As he danced his scary jig

Shaking around the headstones

He spun like a whirligig

40

Much further down

Much deeper in

Before you drown

What's real runs thin

-

A dark facade

Behind it all

A betrayed god

Awaits the call

41

Broken down now

Rot has set in

To live somehow

With death within

-

The heart beats slow

Feebly prolong

Falling like snow

What once was strong

42

No one beside

Nothing to hold

Nowhere to hide

Now its been told

-

Nobody's here

None left alive

Note what is dear

Not to survive

43

As shadows watch over the skies

Consuming chill hangs in the air

Swept up enraptured by the lies

Came face to face with horrors there

-

Our broken land like scattered toys

Torn apart by creatures unknown

A million lost forgotten joys

In darkness lay on what we've known

44

It's torn away

That wasted flesh

Lost in the fray

Blood flowing fresh

-

That gaping maw

Of dripping blood

Left wound so raw

Mixed in the mud

45

Unable to feel

Without hope to see

The horror is real

Buried in the sea

-

Pulled further below

Crushed under its weight

Your death will be slow

Waters seal your fate

46

Remembered dead

Will rise once more

All that was said

Was left before

-

As time unwinds

Death goes to die

Forget your minds

And what's gone by

47

Immortal beast

The lone vampire

Forever feast

Safe from the pyre

-

Demons hunger

Specter of hate

Growing younger

A blood sealed fate

48

To revel in flesh

Freedom found in blood

Sink teeth in kill fresh

And feel that warm flood

-

It struggles to flee

Your claws in its skin

Overwhelmed glee

Fills you from within

49

A tarnished descent

A fearful decay

All energy spent

To keep it at bay

-

But darkness still creeps

The light still grows dim

As sadly he weeps

Sings one final hymn

50

Put fear away

Let go of doubt

Don't let it stay

Please drive it out

-

The dark will fall

And you will die

Despite it all

You still should try

Eldritch Blood

1

As scorching summer sun

Burns marks upon our earth

So too is time undone

Driving away our worth

-

It's too late now to mourn

What's already been lost

When in our world is born

Our judgments final cost

2

What's behind the vale

What watches and waits

Past the mortal pale

Holding all our fates

-

It cares not for us

Our struggles and dreams

We fear to discuss

Worlds not what it seems

3

A god's blood dried

Upon this sand

As angels cried

Waiting command

-

Something far worse

Comes for us now

An ancient curse

Will break its vow

4

Heed these words

Listen here

Like the birds

Flown in fear

-

The end comes

It is soon

Life becomes

Its to prune

5

Can they be said to care

For something far beneath

Looking with ancient stare

Licking thousands of teeth

-

We are but humble food

Insignificant prey

Our world will come unglued

This final judgment day

6

In madness I wake

Walls of my mind thin

It begins to take

To enter within

-

My thoughts are not mine

No longer do I think

My mental decline

Has come to the brink

7

Wretched soulless beast

Past reality

In our world will feast

On humanity

-

It enters our world

It cannot be stalled

All will come unfurled

When were all enthralled

8

Can you feel it

Hear it echo now

An ancient writ

Here to endow

-

All is now lost

Our powers gone

A bargains cost

Forced to move on

9

Ignorance does shield

It protects your mind

For the truth revealed

Should be still confined

-

What's behind that wall

The truth there to see

Will lead to the fall

Of humanity

10

Waters so deep

Waters so still

Above I sleep

I feel the chill

-

What is beneath

Below the wave

Dagger in sheath

Send us to grave

11

From earth stars are calm

A gentle dark night

To them we sing psalm

Praise majestic light

-

But in that dark sky

That endless black sea

Is time now gone by

Lost reality

12

No one remains

Alone at last

Free from the pains

And fading fast

-

Abandoned here

Alone to dwell

A final fear

The world that fell

13

Such devastation

Past reclamation

Cast once grand nation

From lofty station

\-

It's machination

An infestation

Broke dedication

Caused worlds cessation

14

Lost forevermore

Trapped within the cage

Upon fallen shore

Hopes now drowned in age

\-

The voices now quelled

By screaming of wind

Humanity felled

It knows how we've sinned

15

Waiting outside time

Watching million eyes

An infinite crime

Shall blot out our skies

-

Eternity done

It shall consume all

We shall become one

Witness the downfall

16

When gods may die

They're buried here

Angels will cry

They weep in fear

-

It ends the old

Heralds the new

Turns world so cold

Ends what we knew

17

I dream in restless sleep

Loss as sanity fades

And pray my mind to keep

Within these darkened glades

-

Holding dear what I know

Its waves erode my thought

Beckoning to let go

See new worlds to be wrought

18

What does sleep eternal

Hold times forgotten key

To us all internal

Hides inside you and me

-

Hate hidden behind eyes

A step away from doom

Life when the new world dies

Set free from ancient tomb

19

Their dominion done

The roaches scatter

With death of their sun

No plot could matter

-

No power that's held

Within mortal hand

Could save world that's felled

Their broken homeland

20

Long before their reign

It held all power

Their efforts in vain

Can't stop final hour

-

It's come home once more

To rule mortal land

Through eternal door

It shall take command

21

What's rarely know

Yet often seen

A world that's shown

Behind the scene

-

To understand

Before our eyes

What sits as planned

In placid skies

22

A familiar place

Now twisted and deformed

Wears haunting plastic face

For a dance once performed

-

An emptied rotted shell

Of the home I held dear

Awoke from dreams in hell

What I've known now unclear

23

That which I loved now lies

Normal has been shattered

As comfort fades and dies

Nothing ever mattered

-

No safety to call home

Now away veil was peeled

We opened ancient tome

And truth has been revealed

24

Within lies I drown

Under crushing weight

Do they pull us down

Tie us to our fate

-

Or is death in truth

Stories to reveal

Lost innocent youth

Horrors we conceal

25

I ask you what we fear

Already in our lives

That which we held so dear

All that in us survives

-

Or was it still beyond

That which we cannot grasp

Or closer to our pond

Is it that which we clasp

26

Just beneath our feet

Waiting without sleep

Is something we'll meet

Promise yet to keep

-

Pulsing with its blood

Ground will shift and shake

An oncoming flood

Sleepless things awake

27

We ventured too far

Down into the deep

The place where we are

Punishment to reap

-

The things in this dark

Where no man should go

No guiding landmark

Here with us below

28

What brought you here

To venture on

Push away fear

See lands long gone

-

You shouldn't be

Down in this place

The time to flee

You will soon face

29

Soon everything is one

All is reborn the same

Just as when it begun

All held in but one name

\-

All will speak with one voice

Live with a single soul

Now there is no more choice

A final endless goal

30

What we couldn't comprehend

A truth beyond all our lies

No room left now to pretend

We believe truths disguise

\-

What we've seen we couldn't know

Nothing left within our mind

A wretched gift to bestow

On our fragile race mankind

31

A never ending night

Beyond the end of life

A lost and broken sight

In worlds forgotten strife

-

No memories remain

After life's gone away

Our fallen mortal plane

Shall never again stay

32

Loyalty hides hate

Admiration greed

Concealing our fate

Willingly concede

-

The fools welcome it

They don't see what's true

Their end will befit

Their blind naive view

33

Was life worth its cost

Worth unending loss

The innocence lost

When we reached across

-

In nothings solace

In the voids embrace

Is absence flawless

Never in this place

34

Stories left untold

All is becoming

constant creeping mold

A terrible thing

-

Empires once so bold

Are now succumbing

To unyielding hold

As all is ending

35

Is death all that you fear

A simple loss of life

Something worse now draws near

An age of darker strife

-

You will long for mere death

When the world is remade

Fear an eternal breath

Suffering that won't fade

36

Behind our ship

A wake of bones

Our steady clip

Left empty thrones

-

Now to the deep

The empires sink

Forever keep

Now past the brink

37

Resting beneath

Below what's known

Under calm heath

It's slowly grown

-

Laying in wait

Will soon emerge

Our final fate

Begins the purge

38

The gods have died

Sanity broke

The angels cried

As evil spoke

-

Forever gone

Eternal death

A final dawn

Will end our breath

39

We cannot understand

Creatures beyond the stars

Machinations they planned

Existing far past ours

-

Forever they await

Watching they form a plan

Filled with an endless hate

To bring the fall of man

40

Not born of hate

No malice held

But will create

Our doom it spelled

-

Just apathy

Without a care

It absently

Is unaware

41

The end will be slow

Death never to come

Then we all will know

What's revealed to some

-

It's in pain we learn

To accept what's true

As minds go to burn

They become what's new

42

As single cells

Create life's form

It parallels

Our coming storm

-

All will be one

Forever joined

The single done

As all's conjoined

43

It's time for sleep

To just let go

Nothing to keep

No more to know

-

To fade away

Forget the shore

No more to stay

Forevermore

44

Oceans emulsify

Steadily swirl with blood

Millions left to die

Along the shorelines mud

-

The oceans dance and fray

Consuming all we know

We meet our final day

When seen by what's below

45

The flood subsides

Lost in the tide

As pain resides

Still left inside

\-

To drown in dark

Escaping light

Fear to embark

Within that night

46

From what place arises meaning

Is insignificance a curse

Must something be intervening

Are choices we make truly worse

\-

Without that meaning from above

Or if there's an eternal plan

Do deities eclipse the love

Held now within your fellow man

47

Directionless without end

Consciousness slipping again

Unable to ever mend

Swirling void of endless pain

-

Where the many merge to one

All becomes lost in the tide

With what we once were now done

Fragments still remain inside

48

Cthulhu blew bubbles

Down beneath the sea

In r'lyeh rubbles

Swimming there with glee

-

He dreamed of the sky

In his eldritch sleep

He'd watch mortals die

Their souls he would keep

49

That unknown place

That waits beyond

A cold vast space

Out past our pond

-

It's nameless void

So silent calls

All will employed

Won't pierce those walls

50

Perhaps it's here

Our final home

Just hold it dear

And never roam

-

Out past the shore

Awaits the storm

Yet we explore

And won't conform

Monroe's requiem

1

Was it hubris to dream

Was it foolish to pray

The world would again team

With life's dance and its fray

-

To dream beyond sorrow

To feel without remorse

To long for tomorrow

And chart another course

2

Are they broken now

Come from is to was

Curtain call and bow

Without a because

-

Need end have reason

A lesson to learn

Like closing season

A world left to burn

3

There's no-one I'd rather be

Nowhere else I'd rather go

But I can't stand being me

This one thing at least I know

-

Not comfortable in my skin

Always jealous of the rest

But if I were them within

Then self hate would still infest

4

We'll never see you grow

All those years are now gone

Our world will never know

One beautiful as dawn

-

All that you could have done

The person you could be

Who stood beneath the sun

Was lost so none would see

5

From traveled road

A soul worn down

It once was bold

Now bound to drown

-

As sorrows creep

Tears shattered heart

I yearn for sleep

Or brand new start

6

Are all alone

Within our thought

Like complete stone

Without worlds rot

-

Or are we world

Is the world we

Just pointless hurled

No destiny

7

Most are never known

Their names forgotten

Although time has shown

What they've begotten

-

Is memory true

Where meaning began

Or found within you

Part of some grand plan

8

I wish I saw

The way they see

To gaze in awe

All around me

-

But gray and dull

My world now grows

A numbing lull

The beauty froze

9

Eternal lies

There comfort known

A warm disguise

From what were shown

-

Don't wish to know

To understand

What lies below

Comforting plan

10

What do you want

What's worth the fight

Grow weak and gaunt

For what is right

-

Is it noble

To struggle still

To make focal

Some test of will

11

Can you imagine seeing your own personality

A single fractured piece broken free from reality

Lost in the tide nothing more than a casualty

Could it be that my life has become no more than fantasy

-

Is there justification for my morality

Need my life become yet another broken tragedy

Unable to connect thought to our worlds actuality

Nothing but a first person impersonality

12

I wish to understand one thing

Finally somewhere I can stand

Find something onto which I cling

World of more than just shifting sand

-

But trapped here in uncertainty

I fight so hard to only know

That now most inadvertently

All there is left is to let go

13

Is struggle life

Essence of us

Exist in strife

With broken truss

-

Your support gone

Weight on yourself

Become indrawn

Place dreams on shelf

14

Alone in a crowd

Solitary walk

If I screamed so loud

Would they hear me talk

-

Isolated now

But together still

With a whispered vow

The silence won't fill

15

Broken by life

Left here to dwell

A world so rife

With pain like hell

-

Above and below

Nowhere to roam

No place to go

Without true home

16

The door now closed

A tale now done

No more composed

It ceased to run

-

A final bow

The curtain call

It's over now

Like passing fall

17

Nothing ever stays

It's all always new

Ever altered ways

Only change is true

-

Soon everything dies

Soon everything grows

But ever man tries

To hold what he knows

18

Reason makes blind

Knowledge clouds eyes

We come to find

That's why all dies

-

To see again

Beauty once known

Come now and then

New life is grown

19

At stories end

I fear the dark

Long for a friend

Before last spark

-

Requiem sang

Curtain now closed

Final bell rang

Song was composed

20

Survivor alone

After the fall

Here to atone

I lost them all

-

In silent halls

They come no more

Within these walls

I roamed before

21

A path followed

In rusted walls

A home hallowed

But still it calls

-

Abandoned now

Left forever

Like broken vow

Past I sever

22

This is the end

A chapters close

Time left to spend

To the void goes

-

Last echoes here

Resonant call

A single tear

Alone will fall

23

As days fade fast

Forever wane

Never to last

Be seen again

-

To shut that tome

Forget this place

Pen final poem

And leave no trace

24

All in the end fades

No matter how grand

Even sharpest blades

Decay in the hand

-

All empires will fall

Mighty works decay

Soon time takes all

Then all goes away

25

We must let go

Relinquish hold

This thing to know

Forever told

-

How tight we cling

To what is dear

We'll lose that thing

No need to fear

26

Lost stones to dust

Lost life to death

Lost steel to rust

At final breath

-

Lost day to night

Lost wealth to theft

Lost health to blight

There's nothing left

27

Will they forget my name

The path on which I trod

A dusty picture frame

Ground now lichen and sod

-

The road faded to dirt

Footprints lost in the sand

Within our world of hurt

All will slip from your hand

28

To understand now

A defeat conceded

And let go somehow

Ego conceited

-

Finally swallow

A venomous pride

Let it ring hollow

What was once inside

29

To hold but ash

With strength now dust

Unfit for clash

Or lightest gust

-

Shell of myself

Broken inside

Story on shelf

Already died

30

To carry on

And go alone

To mourn what's gone

Hold life you've grown

-

I see my thought

In my own mind

Hope what was brought

Might help me find

31

The live life in fear

Terrified inside

Never holding dear

To a life's found pride

-

All these wasted years

I spent life in vain

So drowned in my fears

And alone in pain

32

As time marches on

And the years slip by

Everything is gone

Everyone will die

-

Lost my shallow life

Wasted every hour

Lived in hollow strife

In fear I cower

33

There was no fall from grace

No tragedy to blame

No enemy to face

But ended just the same

-

A life of boring gray

Wasted confused alone

With nothing more to say

As aching rots at bone

34

No reason left to fight

No effort left to give

I doubt now what is right

Lose sight of strength to live

-

With beaten cloudy eyes

Back broken from the weight

With face cast to the skies

Await my coming fate

35

Dreams have come to die

Forgotten behind

Hopes were but a lie

To have been so blind

-

A promise broken

Whispered to myself

From dream awoken

The thing in itself

36

The tighter we hold

The faster it breaks

The story we're told

Is all the world takes

-

Whether we protect

Or we just let go

It's the same affect

This I'll always know

37

I don't fear the end

As much as right now

The time that I spend

Slipped away somehow

-

The journey is worse

Than it's finale

A long and slow curse

We must wait and see

38

Of legacy they spoke

Time drifted to the past

From slumber they awoke

To face the sun at last

-

They held on so tightly

They bought that blessed lie

Live in silence nightly

In world gone so awry

39

In melancholy gray

In silent longing woe

No longer yearning day

Awaiting final blow

-

It's not enough to end

Dark may outshine the light

Though if I cannot mend

There's no reason to fight

40

With no reason left

No will now to fight

Alone and bereft

Not seeing what's right

-

To surrender now

To simply let go

Or to live somehow

Accept what I know

41

To always fail

No more to try

No tragic tale

Just time gone by

-

No evil here

No good as well

My greatest fear

The gray of hell

42

Why still march along

To a bitter end

To still sing this song

That will never mend

-

To live through a tale

We see where it leads

A mind that will fail

It's own worth impedes

43

The will to carry on

A quickly fading drive

It's safe to say it's gone

No reason to survive

-

To fear every new dawn

And in emptiness thrive

All dreams now long forgone

Desire to be alive

44

Was there ever a choice

Did I hold my own fate

I'm just another voice

Lost as we all collate

-

Decisions beyond us

A rapid rivers flow

We've nothing to discuss

If we're swept up below

45

The end is no mystery

It's not shrouded and unknown

Within our own history

What's next is already shown

-

Now knowingly we follow

Yet still blindly we endure

The coming of tomorrow

In ignorance we're secure

46

Drowned in despair

Drowned in sorrow

Want still to care

Some joy borrow

-

Nothing is fair

Yet still marrow

Comes without care

This we do know

47

Only hate won't end

Forever reborn

To foolishly tend

To those lost in scorn

-

What god would impart

World so lost in lies

To turn and depart

As creation dies

48

Quietly they go

A peaceful ending

Nothing left to know

Far from beginning

-

Nothing left to do

Nowhere left to run

Lost all that was new

Now everything's done

49

The flow of time

Drifts still away

Waters sublime

At close of day

-

The current flows

To oceans shore

To rest it goes

Forevermore

50

A lost and broken heart

Shattered forgotten mind

Destiny for the start

To follow path defined

-

To finally be free

Escape now at the end

To see what life could be

And at last come to mend

Flour Tower Poetry

1

All is sundered

Gods will fail

Eternity plundered

Past mortal pail

-

Sacred shattered

Dashed on rocks

Humanity scattered

By the Bisquick Box

2

From below

Within the dark

The past may grow

From but one spark

-

On retrod ground

Whats lost wont sever

We hear the sound

Now and forever

3

Oh roller mill

Beyond the stone

Through grand will

Your strength was known

-

End of an age

Millstone is gone

A brand new page

The roll lives on

4

All is not lost

The mill is found

Aside was tossed

Into the ground

-

Its bricks lay here

Rough and worn

A past so clear

We still do mourn

5

Through mill design

Wheat was shattered

Through rail line

Flour was scattered

-

Down roads and rails

Cross streams and rivers

Minneapolis never fails

It always delivers

6

Through water power

A mill once ran

The flour tower

A modern plan

-

A tale that's told

For me and you

A mill so old

Is born anew

7

In fields where raised

Empires of sand

Like cattle grazed

From gracious hand

-

A world that bled

Death and defeat

Was finally fed

By Minnesotan wheat

8

In dark concealed

A story lost

The past revealed

But at what cost

-

The lost is shown

Forgotten seen

It will be known

What history does mean

9

In fire twas born

In fire it died

The past will scorn

To history tied

-

Yet life still grows

Its raised up higher

The past yet glows

Reborn from fire

10

Life there is new

Life there is old

Worth very few

Yet more than gold

-

It shone so bright

And yet so dim

With angry might

Sweet like a hymn

11

It corrodes my soul

Madness eats my mind

It extracts a heavy toll

No quarter will I find

-

Within its horrid void

At my mind it knocks

I weep now paranoid

In fear of the Bisquick box

12

It echoes still

The past does shout

A battered mill

Voice lost in doubt

-

Yet clearly said

This very hour

Beyond mere bread

The flour tower

13

We race so fast

The end to come

We hope to last

To not grow numb

-

Yet turned to gray

Once vibrant hues

I long to stay

Midst bygone views

14

We fall in place

We never see

Without a trace

Of you and me

-

Lost to time

Remains unseen

A world sublime

Beneath the scene

15

I here the blow

The burst of light

A mill laid low

By ancient might

-

But from the grave

It rises still

The past to save

Oh Washburn mill

16

Do you know me

Speak of my name

Can you still see

One just the same

-

I was a gear

A piece once new

Removed to clear

A space for you

17

The work is done

Machines stand still

Turbines don't run

Within our mill

-

Yet never lost

Stories of past

Extract great cost

They never last

18

Death is no wall

There's another side

I hear the call

No-one may hide

-

A haunting voice

From beyond talks

I have no choice

Fear the Bisquick Box

19

Histories said

Not set in stone

Nor laid to bed

Here to atone

-

Remembered still

Seen at a glance

Oh Washburn mill

This is your chance

20

History still echoes

What is gone now still speaks

Desires the world knows

What were once lofty peaks

-

In this place at this time

What was forgotten

Will bring new paradigm

Know how far we've gotten

21

The mill grows old

The mill does fade

What once was bold

Becomes unmade

-

But staying here

In hallowed tomb

I still hold dear

Now darkened room

22

All becomes one

Within it's dark

Worlds are undone

An ending spark

-

An elder void

Our world it shocks

All is destroyed

By Bisquick Box

23

In ashes paranoid

Soon all will come undone

With its eldritch void

There's nowhere left to run

-

End of grace fall of man

At our world it knocks

Beyond all mortal plan

All hail the Bisquick Box

24

I sit here alone

Amidst rust displayed

Feels so much like bone

Shells of past decayed

-

This is where I will be

Never more to run

Left here alone to see

Work finally finally done

25

Water to flour

Wheat here to feed

In this tower

I see the need

-

Lost empires bled

Like a fresh kill

The world they fed

From Washburn mill

26

Built out of lime

That sacred brick

A shell refine

By millers pick

-

Built up so grand

A mill so fair

Has become sand

It's shell laid bare

27

With graceful might

It's walls did rise

As if in flight

Before our eyes

-

With gentle grace

As steady hand

The mill kept pace

With strict demand

28

Cadwallader

A man now gone

The great Washburn

He did move on

-

What he left here

For us to find

The world will steer

Its heart and mind

29

We see what's lost

We know what's gone

A frozen frost

We can't move on

-

A temples lies

This alters truth

Neath purple skies

We lost pasts youth

30

Frozen in place

Lost to the world

A plastic face

Will come unfurled

-

Revealed now here

For us to see

What once was dear

Now eternity

31

We don't live then

We're only now

Once long dead men

Speak here somehow

-

Rarely now heard

Voices now sing

An ancient word

Resonating

32

Remembering

What's forgotten

Now withering

What's downtrodden

-

A fractured soul

With direction

Achieves its goal

Resurrection

33

It rises now

Ever higher

Reborn somehow

Even from fire

-

A treaty made

With rotting creep

The mill won't fade

No more to sleep

34

Lines of rail

Veins of road

Tell a tale

Past so bold

-

Wheat like gold

Flowed to here

Past so bold

Became so dear

35

Immortalities edge

There all that has been sits

The futures pasts ledge

Between then and now flits

-

In stories of time lost

Future is awaited

Everythings true cost

Echos seen are stated

36

A waterfall

Cascading rain

Its gentle call

Did heal our pain

-

From beauty came

A world of steel

It bears no blame

Falls once did heal

37

Reborn again

At waters edge

Machines of men

The depths did dredge

-

An ancient fall

Cascading song

A sacred wall

Was used to wrong

38

Ashes ever echo

Words that were spoken

Spoon we will all know

What was awoken

-

What was lost is known

Eternity calls

All is left alone

Even eden falls

39

Under purple skies

Golden grain still waves

Beyond all our lives

After all our graves

-

It's still growing here

Although the mills gone

Like a single tear

Dried by coming dawn

40

From dust comes death

A horrid fire

Like devil's breath

On cursed pyre

-

The flame laid low

It made its kill

A final blow

To Washburn Mill

41

Beneath the stars

Past cities steel

Past hum of cars

And rail lines wheel

-

In place of noise

Shall silent stand

What time destroys

Was once so grand

42

A cities heart

It's very soul

Is torn apart

Burned like coal

-

In nameless grave

A past forgot

We soon will save

Drive back the rot

43

Bread sustains life

Flour becomes bread

To end all strife

All must be fed

-

From hearty wheat

From amber grain

Witness defeat

Of all our pain

44

The roller mill

Gives life to bread

As wheat to fill

Its maw is fed

-

The flour so fine

Flows from that role

Like coal from mine

Now selfish goal

45

I see the past

I hear them now

Its fading fast

I won't allow

-

These things are lost

I will not lose

But feel the cost

Of once grand views

46

Do you hear them now

They all live here still

Their stories endow

Purpose to the mill

-

Though years ever pass

With all their lives gone

From long gone morass

Washburn mill lives on

47

Like permafrost

Time holds us still

Aside was tossed

The Washburn mill

-

Reborn again

This very hour

You all see when

On Flour Tower

48

In Minneapolis seen

A vision of worlds to be

Understand what it did mean

The future they all did see

-

A glimpse in historys eye

Showed things that were yet to come

This city let us all fly

And be what we would become

49

Like long sealed tomb

Forgotten place

An empty room

Like somber face

Alive once more

Where here again

To open the door

Live now and then

50

Not every loss

Not all sorrow

Shall then emboss

Our tomorrow

-

Some things we've lost

Remembered still

Through time have crossed

Such as this mill

The End

Thank you for reading Poetry for Foxes, and/or skipping to this section. Either way you were promised four hundred eight line poems would be contained within this book, and so far that has not been delivered. The first poem in the section "Automated Dreams" was more than eight lines after all. So to rectify this discrepancy the book will conclude with a single extra poem.

401

This is the book's end

It'finally done

No need to pretend

You enjoyed its run

-

If you loved its prose

Found it a delight

Or longed for its close

Thank you and goodnight

www.ingramcontent.com/pod-product-compliance
Lightning Source LLC
Chambersburg PA
CBHW061522120726
48001CB00004B/1385